Courageous Ida

by Ruth Lieberherr,
with help from Anna, Eida, Ella, and Tyler

Copyright © Ruth Lieberherr, 2025

All rights reserved.

Text and Illustrations © 2025 Ruth Lieberherr

Book Layout & Design by carolyn.j.vaughan@gmail.com

ISBNs:
978-1-7328877-8-7 Hardcover
978-1-7328877-9-4 Paperback
979-8-9927055-0-8 Hardcover (German)

Printed in the United States.

Dedication

In memory of my mother, Ida, and all the courageous women of the past who inspire us today. This book is also dedicated to my grandchildren: Anna, Eida, Ella, Tyler. Eida is named after her great-grandmother Ida.

This is me, Eida. I am 9 years old. Ida was my mother's grandmother. My mom loved her very much, which is why she named me after her. I never knew Ida, my great-grandmother, but I love hearing stories about her. I also love wearing the dresses and beautifully knitted cardigans that Ida made for my mom.

A long time ago, in a country called Switzerland,
a girl named Ida was born.
Shortly after, a baby brother joined her.

Another year passed, and Ida welcomed a baby sister!
Before long, there were four children in the family.

"I love my little brother and sisters."

"Laundry is a lot of work!"

More siblings were born, and as the oldest,
Ida helped with many chores. She cared for her younger siblings,
helped with washing clothes, and with cooking.

"I love helping Mama."

Snow sculptures and bunny by Ida's mother— with help from Ida and her siblings

Snowman by Ella (7 years old), Ida's great-granddaughter

Ida's mother worked hard, but she always made time for fun. She sewed dolls and stuffed animals for her children. She played outside with her children. In winter, they built snow sculptures. In the summer, they grew vegetables and picked berries together.

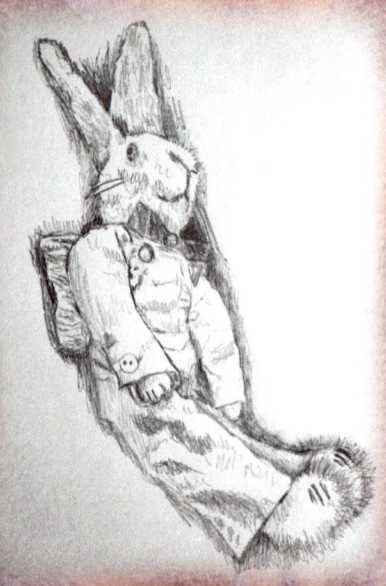

"Playing in the snow is fun!"

When Ida turned sixteen, her youngest sister was born, bringing the total to eight children. Ida slept in a bedroom with her five younger sisters, while her two brothers shared a room of their own. The entire family—and sometimes guests—shared a single bathroom!

Ida loved school, and her parents allowed her to continue her studies, despite the challenges for her family.

Ida became a teacher of needlework, instructing girls in sewing, knitting and mending—skills deemed vital for girls in those days.

She was thrilled to have her own cozy apartment while still helping her family. She learned to ski with friends and embraced her newfound independence.

Then, a great war began, making life difficult. Food, money, and many necessary items were scarce. Ida's family grew potatoes and other vegetables in every corner of their garden.

Ida knitted socks, mittens, hats, and mended the clothes of her family. She was glad she could work, even if she sometimes had to walk long distances in the cold or heat to teach children.

Toward the end of the war, Ida met Oscar, an engineer. They fell in love, married, and at first, they lived in separate countries. Ida kept teaching in Switzerland, while Oscar finished installing the machinery of a flour mill in Denmark. They kept in touch through writing letters to each other.

"I miss Oscar and love writing to him."

"Traveling is an adventure."

After Oscar's work in Denmark concluded, Ida decided to leave her job and accompany him on his next posting—to North Africa. They embarked on an extensive journey, starting with a series of train rides from Switzerland through France, eventually reaching the Mediterranean port of Marseille. There, they boarded a passenger ship, setting sail across the Mediterranean Sea to Tunisia—a voyage that lasted over a day. Filled with anticipation, they looked forward to beginning their new life together in a land rich with promise.

Big Wave by Tyler (15 years old),
Ida's great-grandson

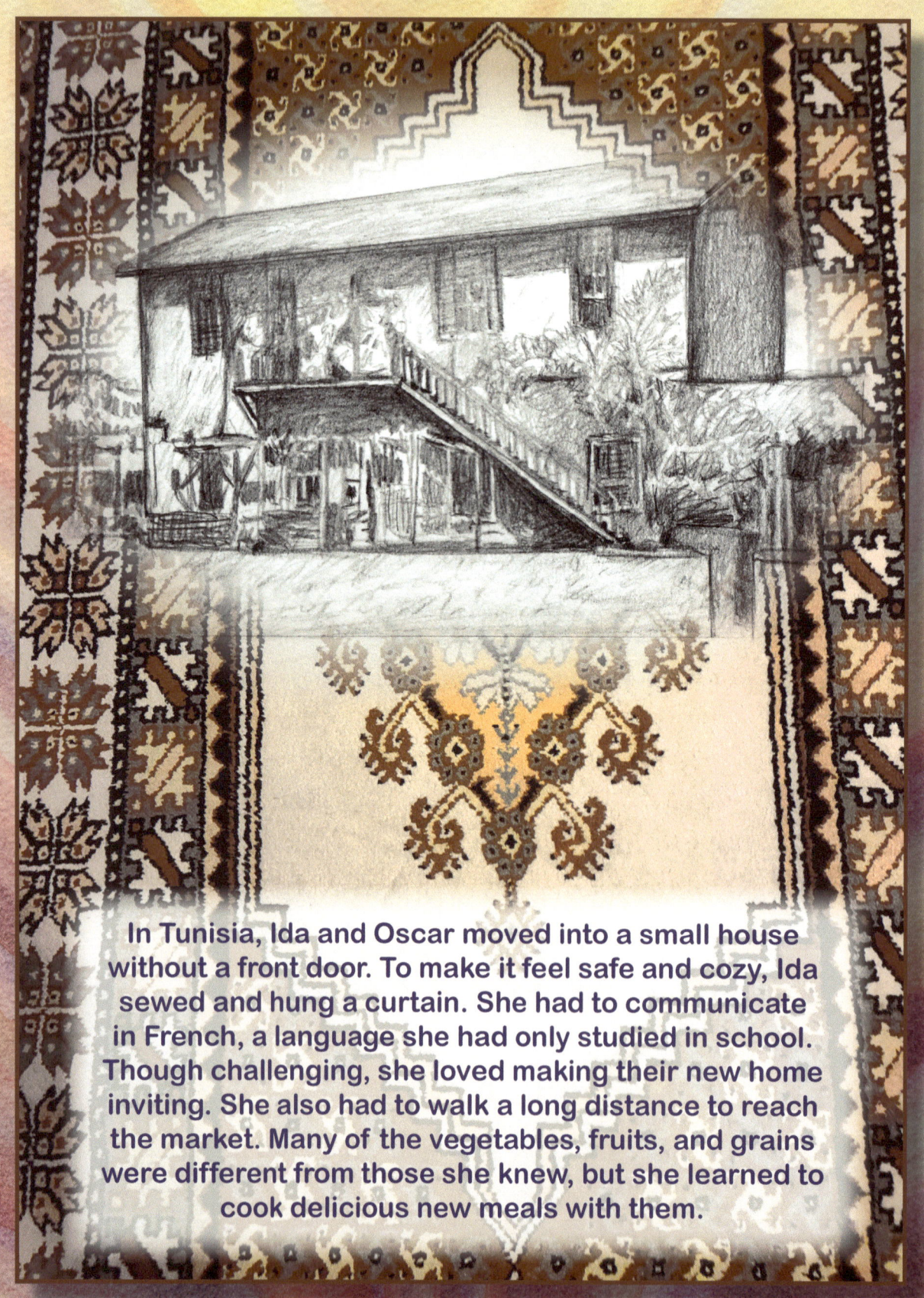

In Tunisia, Ida and Oscar moved into a small house without a front door. To make it feel safe and cozy, Ida sewed and hung a curtain. She had to communicate in French, a language she had only studied in school. Though challenging, she loved making their new home inviting. She also had to walk a long distance to reach the market. Many of the vegetables, fruits, and grains were different from those she knew, but she learned to cook delicious new meals with them.

"Tunisia is different, but beautiful."
"I feel brave in a new place."
"The market is so colorful! It is called a souk."

"I treasure my family."

In Tunisia, Ida and Oscar had two children, Peter and Ruth. Both were born at home because, at the time, it was safer than giving birth in a hospital there. Ida loved her children deeply.

When it was time to move again, this time to Algeria, Ida felt that was too dangerous for their family. Oscar wanted to stay with them, so he gave up his job.
Together, they returned to Switzerland.

Back in Switzerland, Ida resumed teaching. Since her workplace was far, she couldn't come home for lunch, but she prepared meals for her family early in the morning. Peter and Ruth could come home from school and eat with their father, whose workshop was nearby.

Both children enjoyed playing behind their father's workshop.

Ida and Oscar shared many joyful vacations with their children.

Ida sewed an exquisite wedding gown with embroidery and lace for her daughter Ruth. Years later, one of Ida's granddaughters was overjoyed to wear the gown for her own wedding.

As Peter and Ruth grew up and started their own families,
Ida and Oscar were thrilled to become grandparents!

Ida sewed and knitted beautiful clothes for her grandchildren and took them on special outings. The grandchildren loved the delicious meals, cakes, and cookies Ida cooked and baked for them. Ida was a wonderful cook and baker!

Ida and Oscar grew old, and Oscar passed away. Ida was very sad, but she remained strong and continued to live with joy and resilience.

Her grandchildren thought it was funny when Ida fell asleep while knitting and her fingers kept knitting!

"Grandchildren bring so much joy."
"I'm lucky to have happy memories."

Ida lived a long and courageous life, filled with kindness, bravery, and a deep love for her family that shone throughout her journey.

Ruth: Why a Story About My Mother Ida?

After writing about my father, Oscar Kuebler—a "Verdingkind" (foster child) in Switzerland—my daughters encouraged me to write about my mother, Ida, whom they cherished deeply.

My father had to grow up in a social system that exploited Verdingkinder. When I reflected on my mother's life, I realized that her story was also unique. Ida's strength and independence as a working woman and teacher were remarkable—especially in an era when women's lives were heavily restricted by societal norms.

In Ida's time, women in Switzerland faced numerous legal restrictions: They were not allowed to vote, open a bank account without their husband's consent, live with a partner unmarried etc. They even risked losing their citizenship if they married a foreigner—laws that are almost unimaginable today.

Career opportunities for women were also limited. They were often confined to certain professions, such as teaching needlework. Married women needed their husbands' permission to work. Even during my schooling in the mid-1950s to late 1960s, girls were enrolled in needlework classes, while boys participated in 'cartonnage' (cardboard crafting)

Initially, Ida hadn't planned on marriage. However, when she married in her thirties, she fully embraced family life. In 1949, she made the bold decision to leave her job temporarily and join my father abroad. Upon returning from Tunisia, she resumed working—both out of financial necessity and professional fulfillment. Balancing work and family was not always easy. I remember, at age four, trying to keep her from leaving for work by wielding a broom!

Having lived abroad also profoundly influenced both my parents. My mother prepared a diverse selection of dishes, ranging from Swiss to Tunisian cuisine. My parents were open to people of varied backgrounds and cultures, always willing to assist those in need, from family members to recent immigrants.

Like many working mothers today, my mother couldn't have managed alone. My father's support was invaluable, and we also had nannies and household help during my early years. Later, as my brother and I grew more independent, my mother would wake early to prepare lunch, and we all pitched in.

This book is dedicated to Ida and to all the courageous women who paved the way for future generations.

Ida Kuebler-Tyrluch, born April 12, 1913, Zurich, Switzerland; died October 5, 2000, Zurich.

Examples of Ida's Skills

About the Author and Illustrator

Ruth Lieberherr is a Swiss author and artist known for her heartfelt picture books inspired by her family history. *Courageous Ida* tells the story of her mother, while *The Boy Without a Name* is about her father's childhood as a Verdingkind.

Her other works include the picture book *The Caterpillar and the Butterfly* as well as numerous illustrated children's books, including *By Some Great Spell*, *Hafez The Mathematical Stonecutter*, *Journey to Inner Space*, *The Knottles,* and *Winter Awake!*

Her paintings are in private and public collections and have been exhibited in Europe and the United States.

More at: www.RuthLieberherr.com.

Portrait of the author Ruth Lieberherr by Anna (13 years old), Ida's great-granddaughter

Picture Books Written and Illustrated by Ruth Lieberherr
- *The Caterpillar and the Butterfly / Die Raupe und der Schmetterling*
- *The Boy Without A Name / Der Bub ohne Namen*
- *Courageous Ida / Mutige Ida*

Picture Books Illustrated by Ruth Lieberherr
- *Winter, Awake!* (Author: Linda Kroll)
- *Journey to Inner Space* (Author: Deborah R. Cohen)
- *The Knottles* (Author: Nancy Mellon)
- *Hafez, the Mathematical Stonecutter* (Author: Michael Punzak)
- *By Some Great Spell* (Author: Mary Beth Melton)

www.ingramcontent.com/pod-product-compliance
Lightning Source LLC
Chambersburg PA
CBHW041521070526
44585CB00002B/36